Basketball

BY ALLAN MOREY

D1003194

AMICUS HIGH INTEREST 🦴 AMICUS INK

Amicus High Interest and Amicus Ink are imprints of Amicus
P.O. Box 1329, Mankato, MN 56002
www.amicuspublishing.us

Library of Congress Cataloging-in-Publication Data
Morey, Allan.
 Basketball / by Allan Morey.
    pages cm. – (Summer Olympic sports)
 Includes index.
 Summary: "Presents information about basketball in the
Olympics, including the history of basketball, how it became
an Olympic sport, and well-known players, such as the United
States' 1992 Dream Team"– Provided by publisher.
 ISBN 978-1-60753-806-6 (library binding)
 ISBN 978-1-60753-895-0 (ebook)
 ISBN 978-1-68152-047-6 (paperback)
 1. Basketball–Juvenile literature. 2. Olympics–Juvenile
literature. I. Title.
 GV885.1.M668 2016
 796.323–dc23

                               2014045799

Editor: Wendy Dieker
Series Designer: Kathleen Petelinsek
Book Designer: Aubrey Harper
Photo Researcher: Derek Brown

Photo Credits: John G. Mabanglo/epa/Corbis cover;
Associated Press 5; Bettmann/Corbis 6; Bettmann/Corbis
9; Imagno/Getty Images 10; Bettmann/Corbis 13; Rich
Clarkson/The LIFE Images Collection/Getty Images 14-15;
Associated Press 17; Bettmann/Corbis 18; Michael Mulvey/
Dallas Morning News/Corbis 21; Elizabeth Kreutz/NewSport/
Corbis 22; ZUMA Press, Inc/Alamy 24-25; meng yongmin/
xh/Xinhua Press/Corbis 26; Bruce Chambers/ZUMA Press/
Corbis 29

Printed in Malaysia

HC 10 9 8 7 6 5 4 3 2 1
PB 10 9 8 7 6 5 4 3 2 1

Table of Contents

An American Sport

Every four years, the world's best **athletes** meet. They go for the gold at the Summer Olympics. Runners dash to the finish line. Divers splash into the water. Boxers duck and jab. But one of the most exciting sports is basketball. This game was invented in the United States, but it is now a worldwide sport.

Lebron James dunks a ball in the 2012 Olympic gold-medal game.

Dr. Naismith wanted people to be active and have fun. Why not toss a ball into a basket?

Basketball was first played in 1891. Dr. James Naismith wanted a new sport. He needed something kids could play in the winter. It was too cold to play outside. So he tied baskets up at each end of a gym. The kids scored points by tossing a ball into the baskets. Soon, kids all over the world were shooting baskets.

Soon basketball teams from other countries were playing each other. But they could not always agree on the rules. In 1932, the **FIBA** was formed. It is a worldwide group. This group made the rules for all teams to follow. Then teams could easily play each other. Basketball was now ready for the Olympics.

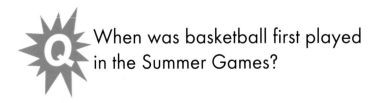 When was basketball first played in the Summer Games?

These men won a tournament to see who would play for the United States in the 1936 Olympics.

 1936.

Athletes and fans filled the Olympic stadium in Berlin, Germany, in 1936.

Men's Basketball

In 1936, the Olympics were held in Germany. Men's teams from 21 countries played. The United States and Canada met in the gold medal game. It was played outside. The court was made of sand and clay. And it rained! The game was a muddy mess. The players couldn't even dribble the ball! But the United States won the game 19 to 8.

At first, not all players could be on the Olympic team. **Professional**, or **pro**, players make money to play sports. These men could not join the teams. This rule meant the best US players couldn't play in the Olympics. So US basketball players came from college teams.

Still, the US team was the best in the world. From 1936 to 1972, the US team won 62 games in a row!

How many gold medals has the US men's team won?

Players from Russia and Brazil shake hands with US players. The US team won gold in 1960.

 After the 2012 games, they had won 14 out of 18 gold medal games.

The US team's luck changed in 1972. The United States played the Soviet Union for the gold. With just seconds to go, the US team was in the lead. The score was 50 to 49. Everyone thought the game was over. But then the Soviets scored a last-second basket. They won the game! For the first time, the US team did not win gold.

The Soviets make the winning basket in the 1972 gold-medal game.

In 1992, there was another big change. Pro players could now play in the Olympics. The US team was called the Dream Team. It had **NBA** stars Michael Jordan and Larry Bird. Charles Barkley and Magic Johnson were on the team too. It may have been the best basketball team ever. They won the gold medal game. The final score against Croatia was 117 to 85.

 Do other countries have pro basketball teams?

Pro player Charles Barkley slam dunks in the 1992 Olympics.

 Yes. Most FIBA member countries do.

US player Anne Donovan fights for the ball in the 1984 Olympics.

Women's Basketball

Women have played basketball for as long as men. But for a long time, they could not play in the Olympics. That changed in 1976. That year, the US women's team played the Soviets for the gold. The Soviets won. They won again in 1980. But the US team took gold in 1984.

The 1996 US women's team was probably the best team ever. It included Lisa Leslie and Teresa Edwards. Sheryl Swoopes led the team. These women became the first stars of the newly formed **WNBA**. The 1996 US Olympic team never lost a game. They easily won the gold medal.

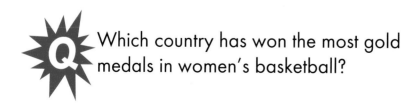 Which country has won the most gold medals in women's basketball?

Pro player Sheryl Swoopes helps the US win gold in 2004.

 The US team. After the 2012 games, they had seven gold medals.

US pro player Yao Ming plays for China, his home country, in 2008.

Today's Olympic Basketball

Many countries have an international team. But only the 12 best teams in the world make it to the Olympics. Before the Summer Games, the teams play in **tournaments**. That's how the 11 best teams are picked. The country that hosts the Olympics also gets to send a team.

The 12 teams are put into two groups. The teams play against each other. The top 8 teams get to play in the final Olympic tournament.

In the Olympic tournament, if a team loses, it gets knocked out. The team that wins all its games wins the gold. The team that loses the final game gets silver. A third place game decides which team gets bronze.

Kobe Bryant helps the US team win gold in 2012.

Players from France and Spain fight for the ball. Both countries have good Olympic teams.

 Why do pro players from other countries play in the US?

In the past, US teams have been the best. And they are still good. But basketball is now a worldwide sport. Spain, Argentina, and France all have really good teams. Their teams include pro NBA and WNBA players. The US teams have to play hard to win the gold medals.

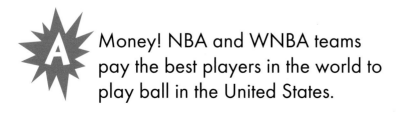

Money! NBA and WNBA teams pay the best players in the world to play ball in the United States.

Cheer on Your Team!

In 1932, the FIBA had only eight basketball teams. Today, more than 100 countries have teams. Every four years, the top teams compete at the Olympics. Players give their all to try to win gold for their country. No matter where in the world you live, you have a team to root for. Cheer them on to Olympic gold!

Pro player Sue Bird drives the ball for the US team in 2012.

Glossary

athlete A person who plays sports.

FIBA Short for International Basketball Federation (or in French, Fédération Internationale de Basket-ball); the organization that sets rules for basketball games played between teams from different countries.

NBA Short for National Basketball Association, the main professional men's basketball league in the United States.

professional, also **pro** A person who gets paid to play sports.

tournament A contest in which winning teams advance; the team to win all of its games wins the tournament.

WNBA Short for Women's National Basketball Association, the main professional women's basketball league in the United States.

Read More

Bobrick, Benson. *A Passion for Victory: the Story of the Olympics in Ancient and Early Modern Times.* New York: Alfred A. Knopf, 2012.

Gifford, Clive. *Basketball and Other Ball Sports.* Mankato, Minn.: Amicus, 2012.

LeBoutillier, Nate. *Basketball.* Mankato, Minn.: Creative Education, 2012.

Websites

International Basketball Federation
http://www.fiba.com

Olympics—Basketball
http://www.olympic.org/basketball

USA Basketball
http://www.usab.com

Index

About the Author

Allan Morey was never an Olympic athlete, but he has always enjoyed sports, from playing basketball to going to baseball games and watching football on TV. His favorite summer sports are volleyball and disc golf. Morey writes books for children and lives in St. Paul, Minnesota, with his family and dog, Ty.